ASK
AND YOU WILL
SUCCEED

1001 Ordinary Questions
to Create
Extraordinary Results

KEN D. FOSTER

Published by: Shared Vision Publishing
Center Pointe Plaza
10300 W. Charleston Blvd. • Ste. 13-227
Las Vegas, NV 89135
info@sharedvisionNetwork.com

First Edition 2003

Visit our web site at: www.ask-succeed.com

Printed in the United States of America

Design by Autumn Lew • Graphic Minion Studios

Copyedited by John Rudin, Wendy Stanley, Edith Fuhlendorf

Library of Congress Cataloging-in-Publication Data

Foster, Ken D.
    Ask and you will succeed: 1001 ordinary questions to
    create extraordinary results / Ken D. Foster.
    p. cm.
    LCCN 2003103491
    ISBN 0-9726030-0-X

1. Success-Psychology aspects. 2. Success in Business.
3. Self-actualization (Psychology)
I. Title.

    BF637.S8F67 2003   158
                              QBI33-1255

Publisher's Cataloging-In-Publication provided by Quality Books, Inc.

This book is available at quantity discounts for bulk purchases.
For information, info@ask-succeed.com

DEDICATION

To All
Who Seek Wisdom,
Wealth, and Happiness

ACKNOWLEDGEMENTS

I would first like to humbly acknowledge my creator and the loving presence that comes through my writings and writes all the scripts in life, the spiritual source of creation within all of us. The gifts that have been bestowed on me by this divine presence are too numerous to list; so I have found that by living in the presence daily and carving my own beautiful life sculpture, I have become the gift I once sought.

I would like to thank my teachers and guides seen and unseen that have guided me through the maze of life and protected me from harms way in all my affairs. I would also like to acknowledge my sincere love for the thousands of people that have passed through my life. Whether my closest friends, family, casual acquaintance, enemies, or someone just passing by; each one of you has shown up in my life at exactly the perfect time and place to teach me what I sought or needed to learn. Each and every one of you has brought me untold gifts of wisdom, healing, compassion, laughter, joy and love; for that I am eternally grateful.

I would like to thank my mother, Edith, and my father, Don Foster, who have given me the gift of unconditional love and the space to ask new questions. I would like to acknowledge my daughters Brooke, Erica, and Tara whose presence in my life has given me unending inspiration and the courage to pursue greater dreams. I wish to express my deep affection and appreciation to my best friend and wife, Judy, for her unending peace, patience and love.

And finally, I would like to express my profound gratitude to Autumn Lew, John Rudin and Wendy Stanley for their unending support and the many dedicated hours in helping me to complete this work.

CONTENTS

INTRODUCTION

This book is designed for truth-seekers who want to empower themselves and others in creating unbounded success, joy and fulfillment in the game of life. The questions in this book are specifically designed to help you discover the values, beliefs and rules by which you are currently living and to help you create quantum breakthroughs in the areas of business, finance, career, health, relationship, family, spirituality and more.

Believe it, at this very moment you are capable of exponential improvement in all areas of your life. Your innate power is waiting to be realized and by following the step-by-step formula for asking and answering these questions, you will tap into that power. You will greatly enrich your relationships. You will deeply connect with your spirit. You will become wealthy. You will significantly enhance your personal effectiveness and you will achieve harmonious balance, happiness and fulfillment. Yes, you will do this and much more by simply asking high-minded questions, connecting with your inner truth and following through with right actions daily.

Why do so many people just settle instead of creating a life filled with an abundance of love, happiness and wealth? There are many reasons; however, the primary reason is that most unsuccessful people live life from the outside-in, rather than the inside-out. They listen to the opinions, advice and counsel of others instead of taking time to realize what is real, valuable and right for them. By doing this, they miss the opportunities life has to offer. Their dreams die, their vision withers and they become subject to a life of mediocrity — just hanging in there listening to what others think is best for them. On the other hand, those who take time for honest introspection notice the trends of their life. They review who they are becoming by the actions or non-actions they are taking. They look at what is working or not and make adjustments with a positive attitude. These individuals are the truth seekers ever looking at improving their life and making a difference in the world.

To become a truth seeker and change the conditions of your life, you must change the questions you are asking. Whenever you ask yourself a new question which is designed to empower you, you will change your focus and consequently you will change your perception. When you change your perception, you will change your understanding. When you change your understanding, you will change your feelings. When you change your feelings, you will change your actions and ultimately you will change your destiny.

Thinking is a process of asking and answering questions. You are constantly engaged in this activity. It has been estimated that the average person has about sixty-thousand thoughts each day. The average person also asks the same questions over and over resulting in same sixty-thousand thoughts the next day. The secret to progress is self-analysis through asking the high-minded questions daily. Introspection is a mirror in which you can sort out where you are strong and what is impeding you.

Learn to examine yourself dispassionately. Find out who you are, not what you imagine yourself to be.

Focus is the key. Whatever you ask and keep asking, you will find the answer. I repeat: whatever you ask and keep asking, you will find the answer. The average mind is like a water soaked matchstick. Scratch it and there is no spark, it will not light. But with the power of focus, a concentrated mind is like a flare. Strike it and it is immediately aflame with creative ideas flowing outward and upward which manifest in the material world.

So what has to happen for you to focus and change the questions you consistently ask? Simply pick a category in the book where you want to improve. Read through each question in that category and note the ones that you feel compelled to answer. After selecting these questions, read each one and as you do, reflect upon each word, its meaning and the meaning of the whole question. Next, close your eyes and allow your honest answer(s) to "bubble up" to your conscious mind. On the surface, it seems like you may be able to answer most of the questions in the book without much thought. However, you will be best served by asking the questions three to five times and then answering the questions after deep contemplation. These questions are generally designed to move you past superficial thinking into a deeper level of consciousness where all answers are found. You will always find the answer unless you turn off the power of the mind by making statements such as "I don't know or I can't." These statements will keep you stuck and turn off the power of the mind.

After contemplation, quickly write down your answers in a journal. (It is a good idea to keep a journal of your answers and commitments to review your progress.) Finally, set a strong intention to make the changes you desire and take immediate action in the direction of that change. Simple, yes! Easy, probably not! It will take focused attention daily to change past habits of thinking and behaving. Just remember, you have the power to change. The spirit of inquiry is in all of us. Everyone in this world sooner or later will seek truth, happiness and fulfillment. This is our immortal heritage. You will seek it either wisely or blindly until you have fully reclaimed yourself. It is never too late to change, improve or mend. "Seek and ye shall find; knock and it will be opened unto you," the great master of truth, Jesus Christ, so succinctly put it.

Remember: the dreams, goals and desires that burn the hottest in your mind carry a message that will help you find your true power.   Just follow your inner compass and it will point the way toward success, freedom and joy. Everything is perfectly aligned right now for you to maximize your potential and live the life of your greatest dreams. It is within you. It is God-given to everyone. So never ever give up on your dreams. Keep asking the right questions and you will make it!

PRAYER FOR WISDOM

Thou hast placed in my heart a great desire to bring forth the greatness that I have within myself. I know that this is Thy desire and that Thou has chosen me as a medium to bring forth many gifts to the world.

I now ask Thee to remove from me every obstacle that hinders or in any way blocks Thy wisdom from coming forth here and now. Supply me with all the means necessary to give perfect expression of my life.

Bring through me quickly Thou desire, thinking, and actions to manifest Thy work for the greatest good of all in heaven and on earth. May Thy will be done always through my work.

ANGER

"I want to know Gods thoughts.
The rest are details."
Albert Einstein

ANGER

What would a life without anger be like?

What period of time have you carried anger?

When are you really going to release your anger forever?

What is the cause of your anger?

What underlies the cause of your anger?

What is causing you pain?

Where do you feel wounded?

What is the source of your greatest fears?

What would it take for you to release your fears?

What is the ideal way for you to deal with anger?

What has your anger cost you?

If you do not deal with your anger, what will it ultimately cost you?

What about ridding yourself of justified or unjustified anger is important to you?

What wants or needs are controlling your life?

Where has anger served you in the past?

Who do you resent?

What do you resent?

What is it costing you to hold onto your resentments?

Who can you forgive today?

What would it take for you to forgive yourself for past mistakes?

What can you do to completely erase the petty things
that are bothering you?

Where has your self-esteem been lowered?

What actions can you take today to raise your self-esteem?

What would it take for you to release your anger forever?

What has to happen for you to find serenity?

BELIEFS

"There is nothing either good or bad,
but thinking makes it so."
William Shakespeare

BELIEFS

Up to now, what kind of life have you created with
your current beliefs?

Where has your greatest thinking got you?

What would you truly like to change or improve upon?

What kind of thoughts do you dwell upon the most?

What questions do you consistently ask yourself?

Where are you critically judging yourself?

What thoughts weaken you?

What thoughts strengthen you?

What do you believe must change for you
to have more success?

What do you do to avoid pain or gain pleasure?

When do you get what you want in life?

What do you truly believe about yourself?

What is the cause of faulty thinking?

What is the cause of blame?

What do you believe is keeping you in your current life situation?

What is really the cause of your current life situation?

If you were to take full responsibility for your beliefs what might your new life look like?

What do you want to change about your thinking?

What old habits of thinking and action are no longer serving you?

What new habits are you committed to developing?

In the past, what has stopped you from breaking negative habits?

What about forming new habits is important to you?

What are your five top reasons to develop new empowering habits?

What will you feel when you master a new habit?

What new beliefs will let you move past difficulties forever?

BOUNDARIES

*"We do not deal much in facts
when we are contemplating ourselves."*
Mark Twain

BOUNDARIES

What are healthy boundaries?

What specifically are your boundaries?

What has been the most significant thing to happen to you as
a direct result of having effective boundaries?

In which areas of your life would you like
to have better boundaries?

Where have boundaries served you?

What is your most effective boundary?

What is your most ineffective boundary?

Where are you inconsistent regarding your boundaries?

Where are you creating pain in your life by not having
solid boundaries?

Where do you benefit by not having effective boundaries?

What are you willing to change to have effective boundaries?

In what ways do your ineffective boundaries affect
other people in your life?

What boundaries have you yet to develop that will
serve yourself and others?

What new boundary do you yearn for in your heart?

Where could you take action to set better boundaries?

Who do you know who successfully balances their boundaries?

What new boundaries are you willing to set and live by?

BUSINESS

"The secret of success in life is for a man to be ready for his opportunity when it comes."

Benjamin Disraeli

BUSINESS

What specifically is great about your business?

What vision do you have for your business?

What are you tolerating in your business?

What are your reasons for being in business?

Specifically, what do you get paid for?

What is the biggest challenge you are facing in your business?

What goals or outcomes are you ready to achieve
in your business?

What might stop you in achieving those goals?

What principals and values would you like to incorporate
into your business?

Where can you dramatically build your organization?

What has to happen for you to enroll key players
in your vision?

What has to happen this week for you to
double monthly income?

What could you delegate to others that would free
up your time?

In what areas can you give more value to your clients?

What qualities do you look for in business leaders?

What can you do to find key leaders?

What specifically can you do to support your key leaders?

What can you do to create a powerful business team where everyone feels they belong?

What is the potential for your business?

What do you need to do to satisfy your customers' wants, needs or desires?

What unique products and services does your company provide to your customers?

When does your attitude affect your business?

What do you really want to understand about your business?

What do you believe the market place really wants?

What is exciting about your business?

What is taking you off track from having the business of your dreams?

www.ask-succeed.com

What are the greatest lessons you have learned
in your business?

What red flags in qualities or behaviors have you noticed when
hiring employees that ultimately have not worked out?

What do you want to accomplish in business?

What is possible for your business?

Where is the ideal marketplace for what you provide?

Who is your ideal client?

What customers do you serve best?

Who believes in you and your business?

What is the mission statement for your business?

What three things get in your way the most in your business?

What decision will you make so these things stop getting in
your way?

What may stop you from succeeding in your business?

What is your job description?

What are the keys to staying motivated?

What amount of time do you want away from your business
and when will you take it?

What can your customers expect from you?

In an ideal month what would your business revenues be?

In an ideal month what would your personal
compensation be?

What are your current assets, liabilities, income, expenses
and net worth?

By what date do you want to grow your business
and by how much?

What can you do to attract more prospects?

What are the boundaries and standards that you are willing to
set and live by in your business?

Who do you appreciate in your business?

What are the signs that you are heading toward failure
in your business?

Under what conditions are you most likely to lose
your business edge?

CAREER

"Do well and you will have no need for ancestors."

Voltaire

CAREER

Is your current career the one you envisioned for your life?

What would you change in your career if you had the courage?

What makes you believe your current career is the one for you?

What is your payoff for staying in your career?

What would the payoff be for leaving your career?

What work would you love to do and feel passionate about?

What career will bring out the best in you?

What does your career mean to you?
What more could it mean?

Where are you disillusioned in your career?

Who do you want to be in your career?

What qualities do you want to embody?

If you could do anything you desired, what career would you choose for yourself?

What is stopping you from having the career of your dreams?

What holds you back the most in your career?

What propels you forward the most in your career?

What is not true about you that prevents you from taking your career to the next level?

Where can you become more influential in your career?

What strengths do your clients and peers perceive in you?

What skills do you want to learn the most to
enhance your career?

What are some of your less obvious skills?

What would it take to include more activities that are fun and
exciting in your career?

Who would be an ideal mentor to support you in obtaining
the fulfillment you want in your career?

What has to happen for you to learn more about your career
and the opportunities it offers?

What are your greatest strengths?

What skill could you develop that would have the most impact
on your career?

What keeps tripping you up in your professional life?

What is currently motivating you with regard to your career?

What do you desire to have in your career?

What do you believe to be the greatest use of your talents and skills?

Why did your current and past employers pick you?

What part of yourself have you given up to work in your past positions?

What do you love the most about your career?

If you could change one thing about your career path,
what would it be?

What benefits will you receive by focusing your attention on a
single career path?

What are you waiting for in your career?

What did it seem like you never got enough of
in your last position?

What issues have shown up consistently in your career history?
Is it still showing up?

What kind of performance from you would attract the position of your dreams?

Where do you want to be right now?

CLEANING THE CLUTTER

"Environment is stronger than will,
but resolve will conquer all."

K. D. Foster

CLEANING THE CLUTTER

What do you like about your environment?

What do you want to change in your environment?

What will give you unlimited freedom and strength with regard to your environment?

What will really make you happy and content with regard to your environment?

What are you tolerating in your environment?

In the past, what has stopped you from letting go of clutter?

What is the worst thing that could happen if you discarded an item and later wish that you had kept it?

What objects from the past no longer define who you are in the present?

What are you holding onto inside with regard to your clutter?

What is it costing you to keep clutter in your life?

In what ways do you benefit by keeping clutter in your life?

Where will letting go of clutter serve you and your family?

What is the most important reason for letting go of clutter?

Who will be most proud when you let go of your clutter?

When would be a good time to let go of clutter?

What can you learn from letting go of the clutter?

What are the five most distressing areas of clutter you would like to be done with now?

What action steps can you take to clear all the rooms in your home of all their clutter forever?

What would you gain by clearing all the rooms in your home of all their clutter forever?

What would you have to give up to clear all the rooms in your home of all their clutter forever?

What does freedom from clutter feel like to you?

What does self-care really mean to you?

COMMITMENT

"He who would learn to fly one day must learn to stand and walk and run and climb and dance; one cannot fly into flying."

Nietzsche

COMMITMENT

What are you currently committed to in your life?

What are your most significant commitments?

What are the highest priorities?

What are the commitments you have set to obtain and/or grow your highest priorities?

What agreements have you made with yourself and broken?

What does it take to pull yourself up and start over again?

What are your primary commitments for the day, week, month, and year?

In the past, what stopped you from honoring your commitments?

What are the characteristics of a person who would be able to easily obtain what you desire?

What would you have to believe about yourself to set goals and consistently achieve them?

At what point do you have certainty that you
are going fulfill a commitment?

What has to happen for you to consistently keep
commitments to yourself?

What has to happen for you to be fully committed
to your commitments?

What does it cost you by not following through
on your commitments?

What areas of your life can you perfect your follow-through?

Why are you determined to follow through
on your commitments?

What would empower you to always fulfill your commitments?

What actions can you take to maintain focus on
keeping your commitments?

What did you learn about commitment today that will help
you make progress tomorrow?

COMMUNICATION

"Judge a man by his questions
rather than by his
answers."

Voltaire

COMMUNICATION

What is the value of being an effective communicator?

What is your confidence level with your communication abilities?

In what areas have your communications been
less than adequate?

What is your vision for the communicator that
you want to become?

What advice do you continue to receive yet refuse to follow?

What areas of communication would you like to improve in?

Where can you use help in your communications?

What is it costing you and others by
communicating ineffectively?

What areas of your life are being limited by your current communication ability?

Where can you apply your current knowledge to become a better communicator?

In what areas can you improve your communication skills and have fun at the same time?

Who are you not listening to?

What are you not listening to?

What confining habits or ways of thinking are blocking your communications?

Who do you most respect as a communicator and what qualities of that person do you embody?

When communicating, to what extent are your inner feelings matching your outer expression?

To what extent do you live what you communicate?

What ways can you think of to communicate that are easier than your current methods?

What has to happen to make the information you want to communicate more understandable?

CONTRIBUTION

"We make a living by what we get,
but we make a life by what we give."
Winston Churchill

CONTRIBUTION

To this point in your life, what has been your greatest contribution to society?

What aspect of society troubles you the most?

If you had the ability to change the world instantly, what
would you change?

Why do you want to create those changes in the world?

Where is your greatest desire to serve?

What are the greatest ways you will benefit humanity?

What is your most treasured memory of how you have
contributed to society?

What new memories would you like to create while
contributing to society?

In what areas can you dare to be different?

Where can you contribute to others today?

What are you creating for society today?

Who are your greatest role models in society and what characteristics of each do you admire the most?

What will it take for you to become actively involved in living your mission and make a difference in the world?

In what ways can you bring greater joy into your life?

What service can you provide that will positively affect thousands of people?

What is the most significant understanding or insight you have gained from society?

What are you saying "no" to that keeps society the way it is?

What could you say "yes" to that would change society
for the better?

What trend or trends in society would you like to change?

Where can you use your knowledge to bring
about this change?

In what areas do you make a difference in the world?

What do you feel when you make a real difference to others?

DREAMS

"We are the opening verse of the opening page of the chapter of endless possibilities."
Rudyard Kipling

DREAMS

If you could have anything at all, what would it be?

What is the most enjoyable dream you have ever had?

Where do your beliefs reflect your dreams?

What can you do to expand your dreams?

What is your greatest advantage in life?

What dream or dreams have you given up on?

What is it worth to you to really create the life of your dreams?

To what extent do you believe that where you are now in your life is where you are destined to remain?

What would you dare to dream if you knew you could not fail?

What do you want to hope for?

What are you willing to give or give up
to have the life of your dreams?

What will your legacy be?

What is your dream for the rest of your life?

What can you accomplish when you dare to dream?

What has stopped you in the past from living the life of your
greatest dreams?

If you knew for certain that you could have all you desire,
what is the first thing you would do?

What would your ideal life look like?

Who can you ask today, to coach you into living your dreams?

What would you need to really believe in to live the life of
your dreams now?

What has to happen for you to expand yourself beyond what
you think is currently possible?

If the range of possibilities for you is limitless, then what is
attainable for you in your lifetime?

What is it about you that makes it inevitable
what is showing up in your life?

What is one step that you can take today to move into the life
of your dreams?

What is perfect about where you are in your life right now?

What does your ideal life look, sound, and feel like?

When you believe that you can't have what you want, what do you know about yourself?

When you believe that you can't have what you want, how do you feel about yourself?

What would it take for you to use your mind, imagination, and emotions to create heaven on earth?

ENERGY

*"Nourish your body with pure foods and pure thoughts
then you will ignite the fires from within."*

K. D. Foster

ENERGY

To what extent are you satisfied with your current energy level?

What compelling reasons could you give for wanting to increase your energy level?

In what areas can you be more productive, energetic, and successful in life?

Where does your energy come from?

What would have to happen for you to have all
the energy you desire?

What strategies do you use to stay positive?

What things are you committed to avoid doing or having?

Where can you learn to face any situations in your life
with maximum energy?

What qualities do people with high energy possess?

What would it feel like to have unending energy?

What must you do to master your emotional states?

What principals do you apply to stay even-tempered?

What are you tolerating that may be blocking your energy?

What are you willing to do to resolve your energy crisis?

What is the best way to maximize your energy level?

In the past, how have you raised your energy level?

What can you do to raise your energy level right now?

What has to happen to rid your mind
of depressing thoughts forever?

When will you commit to stop worrying about things you
really can't do anything about?

What part of your life have you sacrificed by not
telling yourself the truth?

Knowing that anything is possible, what can you change
immediately about your energy?

What about your life do you want to celebrate?

When are you most comfortable with the emotions of others?

What is your comfort level with your own emotions?

What emotions do you consistently feel when you do not get
what you want?

What emotions do you display when you think you will lose
what you have?

What emotions do you not want to feel?

When do you try to avoid strong feelings or emotions?

What has to happen for you to be comfortable feeling
all your emotions?

When do you work hard at not feeling?

When you feel a feeling that you do not want to have what is
the meaning that you attach to it?

What emotion shows up the most in your life?

What emotion strengthens you and what weakens you?

What takes you down when your life is going great?

What has to happen for you transcend the feelings of weariness
and discouragement forever?

If your life continues on the path you are on what will
it be like in five years?

FAMILY

"Turn what has been done into a better path.
Think about the impact of your decision on
seven generations into the future."

Wilma Mankiller
first female Chief of the Cherokees

FAMILY

What do you value most about your family?

What are the most beautiful aspects of your family?

What is working with regard to your family?

What is not working with regard to your family?

Is your family enjoying the benefits of cooperation, mutual respect, and support?

If not, what has to change?

What environmental changes would benefit your family?

What frustrates you the most in your family life?

Which frustrations are you willing to address?

In what areas does your family support you?

In what areas would you like your family to contribute to you?

What needs immediate attention in your family life?

Is there anything you have left unspoken to a family member?

What beliefs or messages did you grow up with that are having an impact on your family now?

What can you do today to increase the quality of your life and those around you?

What can you do today for your family that will matter tomorrow?

Who in your family are you allowing to take away
your energy and power?

Who in your family are you taking for granted?

Is there a single change you are willing to make now that will
enhance your family's wellbeing?

In what ways will that change contribute to your life?

When you leave this earth, what gifts will you
be leaving to your family?

To what extent do you feel nourished and
fulfilled in your family life?

What two actions could you take today to feel
more nourished and fulfilled?

What can you do to surprise your spouse, children,
and friends to make them smile?

Who in your family can you catch doing
something right today?

What could you do today to make your family life better?

FINANCE

"Men are not prisoners of fate,
but only prisoners of their own minds."
Franklin D. Roosevelt

FINANCE

What is your current financial condition?

What is your financial vision?

What would have to happen for you to create the wealth you desire?

What holds you back financially?

Where have you been financially irresponsible in your life?

If you have credit card debt, what is your plan to pay it off?

When will you free yourself from debt and
encumbrances forever?

What does a debt-free life look like to you?

What will bring you financial freedom in your life?

When do you want to achieve financial freedom?

What kind of emergency fund have you established
for yourself and why?

When will you take ownership of paying your bills on time?

What specific income level represents financial abundance to you?

What actions can you take today to change your financial situation?

What is possible for you financially?

Where will you be financially in one, three, or five years, if you continue doing what you are doing?

What beliefs are preventing you from achieving
your financial goals?

What can you do today to start creating a
compelling financial future?

What have you been putting off doing?

What is that procrastination ultimately going to cost you?

What has to happen for you to increase and stabilize
your cash flow?

What would it take to double you monthly income
within six months?

What is your plan to teach your children about
how money works?

When you know you are overextending yourself
what will it take to stop it?

What are your greatest fears surrounding financial issues?

What will it take to create a spending plan that matches your
financial priorities?

What would have to happen for you to make
better financial decisions?

FRIENDSHIP

"Talk to a man about himself
and he will listen for hours."
Benjamin Disraeli

FRIENDSHIP

What specific goals do you have concerning your friendships?

What do you value most about friendship?

What does a successful friendship look like to you?

What have you always wanted in a friendship?

What about you causes other people to want you in their life?

What are your ten greatest gifts as a friend?

Who is your most trustworthy friend?

Who do you trust the least?

What qualities of the person you trust the most are reflected in you?

What qualities of the person you trust the least are reflected in you?

In what ways is your friendship a gift to the lives of others?

What do your friends help you see or understand
about yourself?

What opportunities do you create for your friends to
experience their greatness?

What is your greatest challenge regarding your friendships?

Which habits do you have that offend others?

What do you want your friends to remember you for?

What are you most grateful about in your friendships?

What can you do today to bring real joy to your friendships?

What are you willing to give to have quality friendships?

What are you willing to give up to have quality friendships?

What will have to happen for you to have the quality friend-ships you want and deserve?

When will you experience more fun in your friendships?

What has to shift in you to become the friend you most desire to be?

www.ask-succeed.com

In what ways do your friends influence your decisions?

What do you have trouble accepting in your friendships?

What do you regret or resent about your current or past friendships?

What really matters most to you about your friendships?

FUN

"Believe that life is worth living, and your belief will help create that fact."

William James

F U N

What is your definition of fun?

What about having fun is important to you?

Generally speaking, what amount of fun you are creating?

What areas of your life do you want to bring more fun in?

What is your primary objective for having more fun?

What are your five top reasons for having more fun?

What are you willing to give or give up to have more fun?

When have you had the most fun in life?

When is the last time you really had fun?

What would have to happen for you to create the best
(Birthday, Christmas, Holiday, etc) ever?

What brings you laughter?

What brings you happiness?

Who is the funniest person you know?

What is funny about the way you live your life?

What is the funniest thing you have ever seen?

What do you do that brings you the most fun?

What are the fun things that you like to do?

Where are you most playful?

In the past, what has stopped you from
having the fun you deserve?

What are you willing to move past to bring more fun in?

What tips would you give a friend in your
situation to have more fun?

Who have you let stand in the way of your fun?

When do you benefit by not having fun?

www.ask-succeed.com

What would have to happen for you to have
more fun in your life?

Who do you know that would benefit by you
having more fun?

Where will your life be different as a result of
having more fun?

What would it take for you to totally commit to
having more fun?

What is your next step to having outrageous fun?

GOAL SETTING

"If everybody was satisfied with himself,
there would be no heroes."

Mark Twain

GOAL SETTING

What are the top five goals in your life?

What about goal setting is important to you?

What has worked for you when setting goals?

What has not worked for you when setting goals?

What patterns of action might prevent you from
reaching your goals?

What could you choose to believe to consistently achieve your goals?

What goals have you been putting off that you will to commit to completing?

What is the feeling you are committed to feeling when you accomplish the goals on your list?

In what ways do you benefit by not accomplishing your goals?

What has stopped you from setting and completing goals in the past?

By accomplishing your goals, in what areas will
your life be different?

What new patterns of actions do you need to establish
to reach your goals?

What "incompletes" in your life would a plan of
action help you complete?

Which goals will give you the greatest gifts when
they are accomplished?

What will you realize when you have accomplished your goals?

What do you believe the secret is to setting
and accomplishing goals?

What is your theme for this year?

What has to happen for you to be absolutely certain of
completing your goals?

In what ways would your quality of life substantially increase if
you completed your goals?

What specific areas are you committed to setting goals in?

What is the most important goal you have set and completed?

Who do you know that will help you in
accomplishing your goals?

What goals are you committed to setting that will completely
transform your life for the better?

If you knew for certain that every goal you set would be
accomplished, what would your life be like?

HAPPINESS

"Nothing happens without personal transformation."

W. Edwards Deming

HAPPINESS

Starting today, what future do you want to create?

Right now what can you do to create more of your ideal life?

What does it take for you to be really happy?

What will bring you permanent happiness or bliss?

What will you do to make a difference in someone's life today?

What questions can you ask to empower others?

What are you truly grateful for?

What do you need to do to make your life really work?

What has happened today that has enhanced the quality of your life?

What really matters to you the most and why?

When are you the happiest?

What price have you paid for choosing unhappiness?

What is limiting your life?

When you feel successful what manifests in your life?

What excites you the most in your life?

What are you most afraid of in your life and why?

What has to happen for you to get what you
want in the world?

What are you most proud of in your life?

What are you enjoying the most in your life?

What is the most meaningful experience you've ever had?

What would you like to be feeling?

What triggers your positive emotions?

What would you like to be thinking?

What are the things in your life that you would
do anything to avoid?

Where do you have to be right?

What is your greatest fear about being wrong?

What have you given today?

What did you learn today that could empower
you in the future?

In what areas have you grown today?

In what ways are you a better person today than
you were yesterday?

What did you create in your life today?

What did you deposit into your future today?

After focusing on what makes you happy, what problems do
you have in this moment?

HEALTH

"The time to repair the roof is when the sun is shining."

John Kennedy

HEALTH

In what areas are you comfortable with your health?

What about personal health is important to you?

What has to happen for you to clearly define your health and fitness goals?

What is your understanding of food digestion?

What is your commitment to keeping yourself healthy?

What are your attitudes and beliefs about the food you eat?

What can you do today to create a healthier lifestyle
for yourself?

What do you consider the essential characteristics
of sound health?

In the past, what has stopped you from
having outstanding health?

In what ways are you shortchanging your health?

What causes you to become ill?

What does your body need to thrive?

To what extent do you believe that your body is
the "temple" for your soul?

What has to happen for you to maintain a balanced life?

If you could really change your health what would you change?

What changes are you willing to make now?

What healthy habits are empowering your life?

In the last six months what new desirable habits
have you formed?

What habits are taking away from the quality of your life?

What will it take to make peace with your body?

At what weight are you pleased?

Why might you not perform at your peak ability?

To what extent are you nurturing your body
with sufficient sleep?

What new standards are you willing to set with
regard to your health?

What ways do you release stress in your life?

What is a healthy attitude?

What is the quickest way to let go of resentments in your life?

If you really wanted to become healthy, what would be the ideal resource to study?

To what extent do you like the tone, flexibility, and appearance of your muscles?

What are the most beneficial foods you could nourish yourself with today?

What foods could you eliminate from your life to feel better?

What three activities do you enjoy that will oxygenate and energize your body?

What would your health be like without caffeine, alcohol, white sugar, and red meat?

What thought patterns will prevent you from having the health you want?

What can you do today to improve your health forever?

HOME ENVIRONMENT

"Lift yourself above the burden of your current life
and ride on the wings of imagination into the future.
Imagine your dream home.
Walk up to the front door and step inside."
Mark Victor Hansen • Robert Allen

HOME ENVIRONMENT

On a scale of one to ten what rating would you give your home environment?

What do you enjoy most about your home?

What would make your home perfect now?

What needs less attention and what needs more attention in your home?

What would it take to create the home of your dreams?

What in you needs to shift to create your perfect home?

What specifically would be your ideal living environment?

What do you feel good about in your home life?

What in your home have you out grown?

What do you want more of in your home life?

What will it take for you to create peace in your home?

What can you do today to bring more love into your home?

What has to happen for you to feel fulfilled in your home?

If you knew you could make your home life more fun, what would you do?

What has to happen to create more beauty in your home?

Visualize your ideal home environment. What will it be?

What is perfect about where you are in your life right now?

LEADERSHIP

"Outstanding leaders go out of their way to boost self-esteem of their personnel. If people believe in themselves, it's amazing what they can accomplish."

Sam Walton

LEADERSHIP

Who are five leaders you admire and what are the values you admire about them?

In what ways are you an ideal leader?

What are your greatest leadership strengths?

What level of leadership are you ready to step up to?

What has it cost you to not trust your leadership abilities?

Why is leadership important to you?

What must you face that you have not faced up to this point?

Where will you be prevented from going if you hold onto your current beliefs?

What factors are preventing you from taking on a positive leadership role in your life?

What can reawaken your desire to be what you know you can be?

What will create all around success in your life?

What leadership qualities have you yet to develop that you could use to both help others and serve yourself?

What are the five greatest attributes of strong leaders?

What are your highest aspirations in leadership?

What can you do every day to renew your sense of challenge?

What has to happen to awaken your passion and make leadership a reality for you?

What are the three greatest leadership qualities you want to demonstrate?

What leadership skills are you committed to developing?

What leadership characteristics you committed to developing?

As a leader, what will it take to always align
your beliefs and actions?

LIFE PURPOSE

*"To venture causes anxiety, but not to venture
is to lose one's self....And to venture in the highest is
precisely to be conscious of one's self."*

Soren Kierkengaard

LIFE PURPOSE

What is perfect is your life?

What about life is important to you?

What is your supreme or divine purpose for this life?

If you could create a perfect life for yourself,
what would it look like?

What would you be doing in your life if you knew you
absolutely could not fail?

What do you really want to be doing with your life?

If you didn't have to work for a living what would you love to do?

If you were just given $10 million what would be the first thing you would do?

If you learned you had just six months to live, what is the first thing you would you choose to do?

What do you need to think about differently to have the life you desire?

What are five things you value the most in life?

What are the characteristics of who you want to be?

What are your priorities in life?

What do you value the most in life?

What are you naturally good at?

What makes you unique?

What causes you to wake up in the morning with enthusiasm?

What turns you on, give you thrills, and makes you
feel good inside?

What causes do you have deep concern or passion for?

What things do you daydream about doing?

What is going right in your life?

What matters to you most in your life?

When do you feel most alive?

What are your greatest talents? List ten per day for ten days!

If the future of humanity depended on you and what you do, who will you become and what will you do?

What characteristics would you like to be remembered for?

What would you like your epitaph to say?

What major part of your life would you have to change for you to be alive "on purpose"?

What is your action plan for fully embracing and fulfilling your life's purpose?

What would your life look like if you had permission to be happy and to really enjoy life?

What are you the most determined to accomplish in your life?

Where are you willing to use your power of firmness and unyielding determination to accomplish what you want?

Where can you render the greatest possible service in your life?

LOVE

*"One can never consent to creep
when one feels an impulse to soar."*

Helen Keller

LOVE

When you think about love, what comes to mind?

What are your goals for having love in your life?

What about love is challenging you?

What thoughts do you consistently have, that are getting in your way of having the love you want in life?

Who do you love?

What do you love?

Who loves you?

What about love is important to you?

What would you have to recognize within yourself to experience more self-love?

What will create lasting happiness?

In what areas of your life could you love more?

Where have you been letting yourself down in love?

What does infinite love mean to you?

What about life do you love?

Where has love let you down?

Where have you succeeded in love?

What will bring you unending love?

What have you learned about love?

What is the most important thing you have
learned about love?

What do you feel when you are in love?

When do you know you are out of love?

What has to happen to get love back when you fall out of love?

What can you do to create a loving and harmonious life?

What enchanting experiences do you want to experience?

What captivating moments are you ready to have?

Where have you experienced the deepest sense of love?

What is your greatest contribution to love?

Where have you loved the most in your life?

What would extreme self-love look and feel like?

What would it take to rekindle your love?

MISSION IN LIFE

"Everyone has his own specific vocation in life...
Therein he cannot be replaced, nor can his life be
repeated. Thus, everyone's task is as unique as is his
specific opportunity to implement it."

Viktor Frankl

MISSION IN LIFE

If your personal mission were easily visible,
what would it look like?

What are the ten greatest lessons that you have
learned in your life?

When do you feel most powerful and why?

What gifts do you bring to the world?

What are your strongest qualities?

www.ask-succeed.com

What do you stand for?

What have you envisioned for your life?

What special work do you see yourself completing?

What is it you want that you have not already achieved?

What is your number one goal in life?

What kind of life will you design for yourself?

What positive contributions do you make through your work?

What do you want to get out of life?

What would your life look like if you accepted the greatest good for yourself daily?

If there were a secret passion in your life, something almost too exciting to actually do, what would it be?

What is the most valuable lesson you have learned in your life so far?

In what ways can you use what you have learned to enhance the lives of others?

If you knew in two years you would leave the planet, what would you change?

If you were to leave the planet this day what would you most regret?

What do you want to be remembered for?

What has to happen for you to live your mission?

MONEY

"Questions predetermine the answer.
The size of your question determines the size of your
answer. Few people ask million-dollar earning,
inventing, innovating, generating and creating questions.
They are yours to ask."

Mark Victor Hansen • Robert Allen

MONEY

What would your family say about the way you have handled money in your life?

Over the course of your life how much money has passed through your hands?

What does monetary success mean to you?

When will you make the money you want?

What are your monetary goals?

What resources do you already have that will help you achieve
your monetary goals?

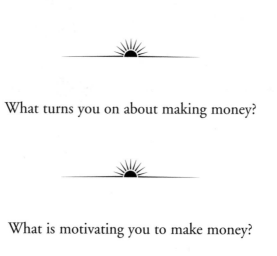

What turns you on about making money?

What is motivating you to make money?

What has to happen for you to create great monetary success
and have fun in the process?

What are the three greatest wealth principals known
in the universe?

What will your life be like when you create the
wealth you desire?

What actions are you willing to take to create the monetary
success you deserve?

What additional resources do you require to achieve
your monetary goals?

When you have accomplished your monetary goals,
what will your life look like?

What is your payoff for falling short of your
monetary outcomes?

What has been stopping you from meeting your
monetary goals?

What must happen for you to be certain that you will accomplish your monetary outcomes?

What will your life look like at age 70 if you do not maximize
your income building efforts today?

What will it take for you to focus on your monetary goals for
your whole lifetime?

What is your plan for accumulating money?

Who can you emulate as a model of financial success?

What are the five most important decisions that you can make right now about money?

What are you willing to give to have the money you desire?

What are you willing to give up to have the money you want?

Where has fear and self-doubt affected the amount of money you possess?

In what ways does fear suppress your essential genius?

What will you do with an excess of time and money?

If you suddenly had more time or money right now how would your life be different?

What is your deepest truth about money?

ORGANIZATION

*"Setting an example is not the
main means of influencing others;
it is the only means."*

Albert Einstein

ORGANIZATION

What about organization is important to you?

What does being organized mean to you?

What is your organizational philosophy?

Why become organized?

What are your greatest strengths around being
organized in your life?

What has to happen to make organization your first priority?

What does being over-organized look like to you?

What things are you not going to do with
regard to organization?

What measurable results will you achieve when you have
become organized?

What excuses are you using to fall short of your
organizational goals?

Where has procrastination fit into your life?

What organizational successes can you create this week?

What are your goals surrounding organization?

Who do you know that can help you get organized?

What thinking can you change inside yourself to become organized in your outer world?

What will it take for you to become organized?

What messages do you send yourself about being organized?

What has stopped you in the past from being organized?

What new belief could create a new destiny for you?

PERSONAL DEVELOPMENT

"Man's main task in life is to give birth to himself,
to become what he potentially is."

Erich Fromm

PERSONAL DEVELOPMENT

What is your plan for personal development?

What are your goals, dreams, hopes, and aspirations?

What are you willing to take ownership of in your quest for personal growth?

What is the best way for you to get started on a path of personal growth?

In what areas of your life are you committed to becoming
more competent?

What are you committed to learning that will accelerate
your personal growth?

What is ruling your life?

What is your typical behavior to unexpected situations?

What is your greatest response to the challenges
of everyday life?

What does your thinking look like to others?

What are you really after in life?

Which of your personal traits would you like to change the most?

What don't you want others to know about you?

What have you never told anyone?

What negative habits, addictions, or compulsions do you want to change?

www.ask-succeed.com

What bad habits do you want to transform into good habits?

What have you been wishing and hoping for rather
than going all-out for?

What do you fear the most?

What else brings up fear in you?

What has to happen for your worst fears to come true?

What could you do in the next two weeks to face
and release your fears?

www.ask-succeed.com

What is true about you that would enable you
to move past self-doubt?

What is the most profound way that failure has helped you
gain an edge in life?

In what other ways has failure served you?

What is the greatest regret of your life?

What do you need to do to completely overcome this regret?

What do you resent?

What are you willing to do to face and release
your resentments?

What voids in your life are you trying to fill?

What do you need to release to permanently free yourself
from guilt and shame?

In what ways have you rejected yourself now
and throughout your life?

What parts of yourself are difficult to accept?

What about yourself have you not yet appreciated?

What are you capable of accomplishing in your life?

What would have to happen for you to smile more?

Imagine you have the ability to see the world with different eyes. What would your world look like?

In what areas have you let yourself down?

In what areas would you like to develop more faith and courage?

What are you committed to doing that will
eliminate your struggle forever?

What are you committed to starting or stopping?

What brings you joy?

What brings you sadness?

What can you accept today that will change
all your tomorrows?

What determines the quality of your life?

What have been your greatest mistakes?

What have you learned from your greatest mistakes?

What is great about your past?

What do you anticipate will be great about your future?

What would it take for you to feel great every day?

Where does your power come from?

Where have you limited your power?

What has to happen to turn your difficulties
into extraordinary opportunities?

QUANTUM BREAKTHROUGHS

"The way to do is to be."

Lao Tzu

QUANTUM BREAKTHROUGHS

What would become possible for you if suddenly
you had no limits?

What limitations do you believe about yourself that you are
willing to doubt?

What will bring you freedom from every limitation you have
created for yourself?

When you truly know that nothing can prevent you from
being free, how will you feel and act?

What will bring you permanent victory in
whatever area you choose?

What is life asking you to do differently at this
point in your life?

What do you believe is impossible for you to accomplish right
now, which if it were possible, would change your life forever?

What is the key to unleashing your greatness?

What resources can you mobilize right now to create massive
abundance in your life?

What one belief could you change right now that
will create unending wealth?

What does the wisest part of you say will create unlimited joy?

What would your life look like if you released all
your self-doubt?

Where can you find the answers you need to get
what you want in life?

What would create ultimate happiness for you in the
next 24 hours?

What areas of your life do you intend to change forever
in the next 48 hours?

What do you need to know to enjoy more freedom, power,
money, and peace of mind in your life?

What is one thing can you make a small change in immediately that will create profound long-term results?

What would it take to create no more pain or suffering
in your life?

What has to happen to celebrate your accomplishments
so completely that you disconnect from who you've known
yourself to be?

What is the next step in your evolution?

RELATIONSHIPS

*"Language and communication
are fundamental to human beings and to relationships.
Language and communication are to us as
water is to fish or air is to birds."*

Layne & Paul Cutright

RELATIONSHIPS

What does your inner wisdom say about your
current relationship?

In what areas of your relationships are you not asking
for what you want?

What aspects of your relationships are important to you?

What are you tolerating in your relationships?

What is it costing you to be in your relationships?

What does it cost your partner to be in a
relationship with you?

Where are you disillusioned with regard to your relationship?

If you do not change anything in your relationship, what can
you realistically expect to happen?

If you could have any relationship you wanted, what specifically would it look like?

What do you really want in your relationship?

What are the qualities of your perfect partner?

In what areas will you have to evolve to attract
the perfect partner?

What would make your relationship the greatest one ever?

What unique things can you do to enhance your relationship?

If everything were ideal, what would your
relationship look like?

In what ways does staying in or leaving this relationship align with your core values?

If you made the choice to stay in or leave your primary relationship, what would you miss and what would you gain?

What would you really like to tell your partner?

What are three steps you can take immediately that will create more harmony in your relationship?

What has to happen to put respect back into your relationship?

If you were to leave the planet tomorrow what words will you have left unspoken?

What do you continue to believe that is stopping you from having the relationship of your dreams?

What is your payoff for not having the relationship of your dreams?

When will you awaken your soul and make your greatest dreams come true?

What are your behaviors that seduce others to be in a relationship with you?

In what ways has your family upbringing influenced
your relationships?

What feelings and behaviors serve as warning signs that you
have chosen a relationship that will not work for you?

What are the warning signs that you are moving into a
disempowering relationship?

What qualities or behaviors do you search for in
potential relationships?

What strategies do you employ to get others to fill your needs?

What are the qualities of a person who you find seductive?

What are you searching for in your relationships?
E.g., money, love, support, etc.

What brings you joy in your relationships?

What brings you sadness in your relationships?

What do you enjoy in your relationships?

What do you wish happened less in your relationships?

What has been your biggest challenge in your relationships?

What is the connection between your spirituality and your relationships?

When you feel angry, what seems to be your greatest fear?

Why did your past relationships pick you?

What is your typical behavior to protect yourself from being hurt?

What do you pretend about your relationships?

What has to happen to reignite your partnership?

What personal qualities have seduced you into unhealthy relationships in the past?

What kind of thinking and behaving on your part will attract to you the life partner you desire in your life?

REST & RECREATION

"It is impossible for a man to learn what
he thinks he already knows."

Epictetus

REST & RECREATION

What does perfect rest and relaxation look like to you?

What has to happen to make your life more relaxing?

What can you give or give up to feel more rested and relaxed?

What creates most of the stress in your life?

When you feel overwhelmed, what is the cause?

What specific outcomes would you like to set regarding rest
and relaxation?

What makes you truly happy and engages you so deeply that
you aren't aware of time passing?

What has to happen for you to feel refreshed each day?

What can you do to make today a special day?

What would happen to your life if you practiced peace daily?

If you could spend one year in perfect happiness,
where would it be?

What old belief can you re-program to give yourself more
peace in your life today?

What new standard could you set to have more peace?

What in your life do you find uplifting?

What has to occur for you to feel more relaxed?

Where can you create more ease and grace?

What has to happen for you to develop a more positive and happy outlook?

SELF-CARE

"Analyze your life in terms of its environment.
Are the things around you helping you toward success —
or are they holding you back?"
W. Clement Stone

SELF-CARE

What are your goals for self-care?

Are your goals regarding self-care aligned with your deepest core values?

What about self-care is important to you?

Where would you like to spend more of your time?

What values are you committed to adopting and living from today onward?

What features would you definitely include in a plan
for your self-care?

What do you do to take care of yourself on a daily basis?

What do people who really take care of themselves do
throughout the day?

What secret dreams or burning desires have you been putting off?

What turns you off?

What turns you on?

What will create serenity and inner stillness in your body?

Where do you find beauty and wonder in the world?

What really and truly matters?

What is right with you?

In your life, what needs less attention and what
needs more attention?

What do you do that gives you the greatest feeling
of self-esteem?

By continuing what you currently do each day, what results
will persist in your life?

Which of your negative habits creates imbalance in other's lives
and your own?

In what areas of your life are you tolerating less
than the best for yourself?

What would happen if you lived a life with zero tolerance
for your own excuses?

What are your greatest strengths and how can
you increase them?

When has worrying paid off for you?

What has to happen to convert your anger into peace?

What are your greatest fears and how are they holding you
back in your life?

What parts of yourself do your reject?

What are the most effective ways you know to move past your
inner blocks?

If you could do anything you wanted without restrictions,
what would it be?

If you gave up worrying about what others say, think, or feel
what would your life be like?

What will you gain by using your inner courage to take great
care of yourself?

What new actions could you take on a regular basis that would
make a tremendous difference in the way you feel?

SPIRITUAL

"Cut loose your consciousness from the body.
Use it no more as an excuse to accept limitations."
Parmahansa Yogananda

SPIRITUAL

Why were you born on this planet in this period of time?

What do you yearn for in the deepest part of your soul?

What were you born to do?

What is your quest in life?

Where are you going from here?

What have you learned about the other side?

Where have you limited the unlimited?

What can you do to deepen your experience of God?

If you could devise the best strategy for your spiritual evolution, what would it be?

What are your goals for connecting with God?

What insights do you have about why you were created?

What have you always known to be true in your life?

What does the experience of God feel like?

Is there anything that seems to lessen your feeling of God?

What is God's dream for your life?

What five ways can you increase your faith?

What can you do to make love's presence be felt more
strongly within your world?

What are the three most powerful spiritual principals you are committed to learning?

What do you want to proclaim to the universe?

Who are you becoming?

What is your highest vision of God?

Who is your self?

What do you know about your real self?

What, if anything, does God want from you?

What threads connect everything in the universe?

What would your life be like if you didn't have
negative memories?

What are the most useful, empowering, and inspiring outcomes of your relationship with God?

What can you do for God today?

What has to happen to feel a deeper love for your creator?

What is the best way for you to remember and tune into
the sacred daily?

What is the easiest way to increase your wisdom?

What could you do with even more energy and enthusiasm in
your spiritual life?

What would it take for you to know that there are no limits to
what you can do with your life?

What does universal love mean to you?

What does unconditional love mean to you?

What is the essence of your being?

What has to happen for you to consciously connect with your wise self on a daily basis?

In what areas can you become more creative?

What can you do to move past the fear of defeat forever?

What is the greatest lesson death can teach you?

Where does the light of God shine in your life?

What would you like God to say to you?

SUCCESS

"It's not whether you get knocked down;
it's whether you get up."
Vince Lombardi

SUCCESS

What accomplishments must occur for you to conclude that your life was satisfying and well lived?

What will it take for you to accomplish anything you desire?

What is your track record for getting what you want in life?

What magnificent successes will you create this year?

What about success is important to you?

When do you feel most successful and why?

Where in your life do you get the results you seek?

What is the greatest lesson you have learned about success?

What belief would create more success in your endeavors?

If you are not happy with the results you're getting, what are you willing to change?

When you become determined to achieve your goals, what happens?

www.ask-succeed.com

What are the personal issues or challenges that are repeatedly
blocking your successes?

What is the payoff for not accomplishing the goals
you've set for yourself?

What messages have you been sending yourself
regarding your success?

What fears have stopped you from succeeding in the past?

What is really stopping you from fulfilling your goals?

If you fail to improve or change, what will it
ultimately cost you?

What would someone who really expects to succeed be doing
without a doubt?

What would you need to believe to be successful right now?

What qualities do you display to the world when
you are successful?

What really defines success for you?

What will your fear of success ultimately cost you?

What would it take for you to increase your desire for success?

What must happen for you to incorporate successful traits in your life?

What is your strategic plan to get started on a successful path in your life?

What questions do you ask yourself that disempower you?

What might you do today, that in the past you
thought was impossible?

What beliefs have been holding you back in your life?

What are the things in life you would do anything to avoid?

What can you focus on to keep positive thoughts running
through your mind?

What haven't you done that is creating anxiety in
your life now?

What are the pleasures that you link to the pain of inaction?

What price will you ultimately pay if you don't
make changes now?

What would it take to trust yourself to succeed?

What do you already know that assures you will be successful?

If there were something new that you needed to know to be
successful, what would it be?

What opens up your creativity?

What are the signs that you are heading down the path of failure?

Who can you meet today that will make a massive change in your success?

What does it take to change your attitude instantly?

What is possible for you if you no longer waver in your choices?

What actions can you take to silence your discordant or negative thoughts forever?

What can you do to transform your problems into solutions?

If you chose to think successful thoughts every moment, how would your life be different?

If you stopped running your life based on what others thought about you, what would your life be like?

If you were not afraid of death, how would you live your life?

If you released your fear of losing anything, how would you live your life and what new risks would you be willing to take?

If you were willing to ask for what you need, what would your life be like?

If you were not afraid to say "yes" or "no" to anything or anyone, what would your life be like?

What does your life look like when it is working the way you want?

What will you do today prepare for success tomorrow?

Where have you been invincible and victorious in your life?

What would you do with your life if you were brave?

If you believed that you are perfect just the way you are, how would you live your life?

TIME

"Modern man thinks he loses something—time—when he does not do things quickly. Yet he does not know what to do with the time he gains—except kill it."

Erich Fromm

TIME

What is your definition of time?

In the next five years where do you plan to spend most
of your time?

What shows up when you are managing your
time appropriately?

What do you waste time on?

What are your highest priorities on a daily basis?

What are five effective ways you could create
more time for yourself?

What is your strategy for creating more time for yourself?

What is the best use of your time right now?

What is the number one time management skill you are
currently benefiting from?

What new and significant time management skill could you
begin using right now?

What has to happen for you to be more efficient
with your time?

What results would you expect by managing your time
more effectively?

What is the payoff when you do not manage your
time effectively?

In what ways do you limit the time you have to spend on what
you really love doing?

Where does it serve you to limit the time you spend doing
what you love?

What can you do to improve your time management skills?

In what ways do you use time to serve you?

What will it take to be more proactive and influential in mastering your time?

What amount of time do you spend living in the past or future?

Where are you disempowering yourself by making poor time management decisions?

What do you fear about time?

What is it about time that works for you?

When you are not managing your time effectively,
how do you feel?

Where are you giving away your time?

What has to happen in your life for you to be
"in the flow" with time?

TRAVEL

"Well done is better than well said."

Ben Franklin

TRAVEL

What are your travel goals?

Why do you want to travel?

What are you willing to give or give up to accomplish these goals?

What are your beliefs about traveling when and where you want?

What has prevented you from accomplishing your travel goals?

What is your excuse for not traveling where you want?

Why is travel important to you?

What do you get out of traveling?

What are the five most important things you have learned while traveling?

What benefits do you receive by traveling?

Where in your heart do you long to travel?

Who would you like to travel with?

What travel opportunities are available to you now?

What will it take for you to travel more in your life?

What are you waiting for?

What are three steps that you can take immediately to accomplish your travel goals?

What is your strategy for fulfilling your travel goals?

What are three steps you can take this week that will guarantee
your travel goals become reality?

VALUES CLARIFICATION

*"Real education consists of
drawing the best out of yourself."*
Mahatma Mohandas Ghandi

VALUES CLARIFICATION

What do you value in life?

What do you desire the most in your life?

What do you love the most in your life?

What empowers you?

What do you hold dear in life?

What do you enjoy?

What gives you a sense of freedom?

What do you want to have?

What do you want to be?

What do you want to do?

Where do you lie to yourself and others?

Where do you withhold the truth?

Where do you find integrity missing in you life?

What do you need to live your values on a daily basis?

What do you value the most?

What are your five top values and what is most important to
you about each one?

What has to happen for you to live your top five values
on a daily basis?

What is important about knowing your values?

When you know your values what will you know about yourself?

What is your favorite word?

When do you enjoy yourself the most?

Where is your courage found?

THE ONLY REMAINING QUESTIONS

"Without vision, the people perish."

Proverbs 29:18

THE ONLY
REMAINING QUESTIONS

Based on what you have learned about yourself, who are you?

Where truly does the source of your power reside?

Who do you know that would benefit by asking
these questions?

WHAT'S NEXT?

If you would like to find out more about
creating success in all areas of life and continue your adventure
into the world of self-discovery, please join Ken Foster and
other great thinkers for hands-on coaching, workshops,
and learning at:

www.ask-succeed.com
Or e-mail
Info@Ask-Succeed.com

Also to join other like-minded individuals who are growing
their lives and businesses through master-mind groups, and
live events with nationally-known authors, speakers
and business leaders visit:

www.sharedvisionnetwork.com

WE ARE LISTENING!

We would love to hear how this book has affected your life and the lives of those around you. We encourage you to share your insights and stories. If you have a tip or a quote that you would like to share, please send it to us. With your permission, we will put these insights and tips on our web site to help others grow in their lives. Please e-mail us at: contactus@ask-succeed.com or visit our web site www.ask-succeed.com.

WE ARE GIVING!

Ken is currently offering a FREE personalized Coaching Session for everyone who has purchased this book and is serious about improving, changing or developing their life to the fullest extent. You will receive a FREE Coaching Session with a Premier Coach as our way of saying, "Thank you." This is a limited offer and we reserve the right to cancel this offer at any time. To take advantage of this offer go to www.ask-succeed.com and sign up or e-mail us at contactus@ask-succeed.com and we will send you materials to get you started.

WE ARE SUPPORTING!

To grow your vision and live an outstanding life, you will need to ask bigger questions, dream bigger, turn your dreams into goals, resolve to accomplish those goals, and take daily focused actions. You will also need a support team. To this end, we recommend you find a coach or mentor and a networking group. To do life alone is boring, dull and glum! Go to www.sharedvisionnetwork.com and grow your business by networking your way to success with people who are making a difference.